Sports Illustrated KIDS

GAME-CHANGING COACHES

HOCKEY'S BEST COACHES

Influencers, Leaders, and Winners on the Ice

written by Shane Frederick

CAPSTONE PRESS
a capstone imprint

Published by Capstone Press, an imprint of Capstone
1710 Roe Crest Drive, North Mankato, Minnesota 56003
capstonepub.com

Library of Congress Cataloging-in-Publication Data
Names: Frederick, Shane, author.
Title: Hockey's best coaches : influencers, leaders, and winners on the ice / by Shane Frederick.
Description: North Mankato, Minnesota : Capstone Press, 2024. | Series: Sports illustrated kids. Game-changing coaches | Includes bibliographical references and index. | Audience: Ages 8-11 | Audience: Grades 4-6 | Summary: "Sometimes a hockey team's best member is on the bench, not the ice. From college to the pros to the Olympics, learn about hockey's legendary leaders. Who has won the most Stanley Cup championships? Which college coach handpicked a team that made an Olympic miracle happen? Turn these pages to find out!" — Provided by publisher.
Identifiers: LCCN 2023027775 (print) | LCCN 2023027776 (ebook) | ISBN 9781669063483 (hardcover) | ISBN 9781669063667 (paperback) | ISBN 9781669063520 (pdf) | ISBN 9781669063674 (epub) | ISBN 9781669063681 (kindle edition)
Subjects: LCSH: Hockey coaches—Juvenile literature. | Hockey—Coaching—Juvenile literature.
Classification: LCC GV847.25 .F737 2024 (print) | LCC GV847.25 (ebook) | DDC 796.962—dc23/eng/20230713
LC record available at https://lccn.loc.gov/2023027775
LC ebook record available at https://lccn.loc.gov/2023027776

Editorial Credits
Editor: Mandy Robbins; Designer: Dina Her; Media Researcher: Jo Miller; Production Specialist: Tori Abraham

Image Credits
Associated Press, 8, 10, 15, 19, Bill Kostroun, 14, Carlos Osorio, 7, Chuck Stoody, CP, 9, Richard Drew, 11; Getty Images: Bruce Bennett, Cover, (top right), 5, 13, 16, 21, 22, George Peters, design element (throughout), Rick Stewart, 27, 28, Steve Powell, 25; Shutterstock: Adam Vilimek, Cover, (middle), aperturesound, Cover, (bottom right), EV040, Cover, design element, inspiring.team, Cover, design element, Kobzev Dmitry, Cover, (bottom right) background, Luxury_Studio, design element (throughout), Milano M, design element (throughout), rustamank, Cover, (top left); Sports Illustrated: David E. Klutho, Cover, (bottom left), 17, 26

All internet sites appearing in back matter were available and accurate when this book was sent to press.

Printed and bound in the USA. 5626

TABLE OF CONTENTS

Words in **BOLD** are in the glossary.

INTRODUCTION

THE BENCH BOSSES

Hockey players make the plays out on the ice. But the difference between a good team and a great team often comes down to coaching. The right coach can be a game changer for a **franchise**.

In November 2018, the St. Louis Blues found themselves at the bottom of the National Hockey League (NHL) standings. The team made a coaching change. They brought up assistant coach Craig Berube to lead the way. Something clicked, and by June 2019, the Blues were **Stanley Cup** champions.

Different coaches have different effects on their teams. Some have strengths in managing players and building teams. Some are master motivators. Others completely change the way the game is played. The best coaches do all of those things. They also rack up the wins and—if they're really good—championships.

Craig Berube holds up the Stanley Cup after leading the Blues to victory in 2019.

CHAPTER 1

THE BEST OF THE BEST

No NHL coach has won more than Scotty Bowman. Over 30 years, Bowman coached five teams—the St. Louis Blues, Montreal Canadiens, Buffalo Sabres, Pittsburgh Penguins, and Detroit Red Wings. In total, those teams won 1,244 regular season games with Bowman running the bench.

During the 1995–96 season, Bowman led Detroit to an NHL record. The Red Wings won 62 games that season. They broke the old record of 60 wins set by Montreal in 1976–77. Guess who coached that team? That's right—Scotty Bowman!

Bowman was also a championship coach. He led his teams to nine Stanley Cups—more than any other coach.

Scotty Bowman gives the ref a piece of his mind.

Fact

The Stanley Cup is the oldest trophy in North American sports. It was first awarded in 1893.

Canadiens players carry Hector Blake after winning the Stanley Cup.

No coach won more Stanley Cups with a single team than Hector "Toe" Blake. He led the Montreal Canadiens to eight championships between 1956 and 1968. Blake was a **Hall of Fame** player before he moved behind the bench. He won titles in each of his first five seasons as coach.

Clarence Henry "Happy" Day, also known as "Hap" Day, ranks third in Stanley Cups. He led the Toronto Maple Leafs to five championships between 1942 and 1949. To win that first Cup, Day's team had to make an amazing comeback. The Red Wings won the first three games of the best-of-seven series. The Maple Leafs rallied to win the next four. That's the only time that has happened in the history of the Stanley Cup Finals.

Where's Stanley?

Who is the best coach to never win a Stanley Cup? Alain Vigneault ranks 10th in all-time wins. He had 722 victories over 20 seasons with the Canadiens, Canucks, Rangers, and Flyers. He took Vancouver and New York to the Stanley Cup Finals but never won it.

Alain Vigneault

George Imlach celebrates winning the 1962 Stanley Cup with his players.

The NHL recognizes nine **dynasties** in the history of the league. Dynasties are teams that have won several Stanley Cups in a row or many over a short period of time. Toe Blake's Canadiens and Hap Day's Maple Leafs were dynasties, of course. But they were not the only ones.

The Maple Leafs built another dynasty in the 1960s, thanks to the coaching of George "Punch" Imlach. Toronto won four championships in six seasons, including three in a row from 1962 to 1964.

Al Arbour was part of the Leafs' three-peat as a player. But as a coach, he did one better. Arbour led the New York Islanders to four Stanley Cup titles in a row from 1980 to 1983.

Glen Sather and the Edmonton Oilers picked up right where the Islanders left off. They had unstoppable superstar Wayne Gretzky leading the way. Sather's teams won five Cups in seven years, starting in 1984.

Al Arbour shakes hands with Gord Dineen.

CHAPTER 2

GETTING INTO THE GAME

PLAYER-COACHES

Many coaches move behind the bench after their NHL playing careers end. But some don't make it to the NHL until they become coaches. Colorado Avalanche coach Jared Bednar played and coached in the minor leagues. He finally got his shot in the NHL in 2022. Bednar led the Avalanche to a Stanley Cup championship.

Six of the seven Sutter brothers from Alberta, Canada, made it to the NHL as players. Four of them went on to become head coaches. Three of those brothers, Brian, Brent, and Darryl, each coached the Calgary Flames for a time. Darryl Sutter coached the Flames two different times. In between, he led the Los Angeles Kings to Stanley Cup titles in 2012 and 2014.

Jared Bednar celebrates the 2022 Stanley Cup win with his team.

Many Hall of Fame players have gone on to become head coaches, some of them quite successfully. These include Hap Day and Toe Blake. Canadiens star Jacques Lemaire was another Hall-of-Famer turned coach. He guided the New Jersey Devils to a title in 1995. The best player of all time, Wayne Gretzky, gave coaching a try too. He was part owner of the Phoenix Coyotes at the time. Gretzky was known as "The Great One" when he played, but his coaching wasn't so great. He lasted four seasons and lost more games than he won.

Jacques Lemaire instructs his players.

Put Yourself In, Coach!

Lester Patrick was the New York Rangers first coach. He led them to two Stanley Cups. During a playoff game in 1927, the Rangers goaltender was injured. There were no backup goalies then. So 44-year-old Patrick put on the goalie's gear and finished the game in the net. The Rangers won in overtime!

Lester Patrick (center) celebrates the Rangers' 1940 Stanley Cup win.

Jon Cooper draws up a play.

COACHES ONLY

Some coaches rise to the top even without playing much beyond their teenage years. Jon Cooper of the Tampa Bay Lightning did not play hockey past high school. In fact, he played lacrosse in college. After college, Cooper went to law school. After realizing he didn't like being a lawyer, he tried coaching. Eventually, Cooper earned positions at the junior and minor-league levels before getting hired in Tampa in 2013. In 2020 and 2021, Cooper led the Lightning to back-to-back Stanley Cup championships.

Ken Hitchcock began coaching when he was working as a hockey equipment salesman in the city of Edmonton in Alberta, Canada. His team of high school-age players was very successful. That success led to new opportunities. In 1999, he coached the Dallas Stars to a Stanley Cup championship. He went on to coach several other NHL teams.

Ken Hitchcock is deep in thought during a 2012 St. Louis Blues game.

CHAPTER 3

MAKING THE GAME BETTER

The game of hockey has **evolved** a lot since it was first invented. Coaches have played a big part in refining the game. That includes changing rules, coming up with creative ideas within the rules, or doing things to better develop their players.

In 1931, Art Ross, coach of the Boston Bruins, decided to pull his goalie off the ice. His team was losing near the end of a game, so he called his goaltender to the bench and sent an extra attacker out on the ice. That way the team could give itself a better chance to tie the game before it ended. This once unheard-of tactic happens regularly today.

Art Ross shakes hands with Boston Bruins player Eddie Shore.

Roger Neilson coached eight different teams between 1977 and 2002. He was known as "Captain Video." Neilson was the first coach to regularly use video to scout and study other teams. Doing this helped him plan for games. He also used it as a teaching tool for his own players.

Today, most teams employ multiple assistant coaches, a goaltending coach, and a coach devoted to video. Today's coaches can be seen on the bench looking at iPads and tablets to watch instant replays and immediately determine why a certain play happened in a game.

Fact

In 1972, Fred "the Fog" Shero of the Philadelphia Flyers became the first coach to hire a full-time assistant coach. He chose Mike Nykoluk.

J.T. Compher and Matt Nieto of the Colorado Avalanche use a tablet on the bench.

The Jack Adams Award

HONORING THE BEST

Every year since 1974, the NHL has presented the Jack Adams Award to the league's coach of the year. Jack Adams coached the Detroit Red Wings for 20 years. That includes early seasons when the team was known as the Cougars and then the Falcons. He won 413 games before stepping down in 1947.

Pat Burns won the award three times with three different teams. They were the Canadiens (1989), Maple Leafs (1993), and Bruins (1998). Four coaches have won the award twice, including the Red Wings' Jacques Demers. He was the only coach to win it in back-to-back seasons in 1987 and 1988.

CHAPTER 4

OUTSIDE THE NHL

MIRACLE MAN

In 1980, coach Herb Brooks led Team USA's men's ice hockey team to the greatest upset in Olympic sports history. It has been called the "Miracle on Ice." Team USA, which was mostly made up of college players, won the gold medal. They defeated the mighty, experienced Russian team from the **Soviet Union** along the way. The Soviets had won the previous four Olympic golds and went on to win the next three.

Brooks was demanding. He pushed his players beyond their limits. But he was also **inspirational**. Before playing the Soviets, Brooks told his team:

"You were born to be a player. You were meant to be here. This moment is yours."

Team USA celebrates their 1980 Olympic win over the Soviet Union.

Brooks was also a successful college coach at the University of Minnesota and coached four NHL teams. In 1998 he coached France's Olympic team. But 22 years after the "Miracle on Ice," he coached a U.S. team made up of NHL players to a silver medal at the 2002 Olympics.

Fact

Anatoly Tarasov was known as "the father of Russian hockey." He built the powerful "Red Army" team by combining **finesse**, toughness, and physical fitness.

THE COLLEGE GAME

College hockey is a popular sport in many parts of the United States, especially the Midwest and Northeast. The top teams are led by some great coaches. The all-time winner in the college game is Jerry York. He won 1,123 games over 50 years with Clarkson, Bowling Green, and Boston College. The Hockey Hall of Famer's teams won five National Collegiate Athletic Association (NCAA) championships. Four of the five titles were won at Boston College.

Vic Heyliger won the most national titles. He guided the University of Michigan to six championships in the 1940s and 1950s.

Jerry York celebrates leading Boston College to the 2010 NCAA Championship.

Bob Johnson gets heated during a 1990 Pittsburgh Penguins game.

"Badger Bob" Johnson of the University of Wisconsin was one of the first U.S. college coaches to move on to the NHL. After winning three championships with the Badgers in the late 1970s and early '80s, he won a Stanley Cup with the Pittsburgh Penguins in 1991.

Fact

The all-time winningest coach at the Canadian major junior level is Brian Kilrea. He won 1,194 games with the Ottawa 67's, including one game on his 80th birthday in 2014.

WOMEN GETTING IN THE GAME

College hockey has given rise to women's hockey. Women have coached many college teams. Shannon Miller took the University of Minnesota–Duluth to five NCAA titles. She led Team Canada to a silver medal in 1998. Nadine Muzerall helped make the Ohio State Buckeyes national champions in 2022.

NHL teams have hired female coaches too. Dawn Braid was the first full-time female coach. She was hired as a skating coach by the Arizona Coyotes in 2016. In 2022, the Washington Capitals promoted Emily Engel-Natzke to full-time video coach. The game of hockey is always changing, and coaches are a big reason why.

Shannon Miller speaks with Team Canada players during a 1997 game.

TIMELINE

1917	The National Hockey League is formed.
1920–1927	Ottawa Senators dynasty
1931	Art Ross becomes the first coach to pull the goalie.
1947–1951	Toronto Maple Leafs first dynasty
1948	Michigan wins the first NCAA hockey championship.
1950–1955	Detroit Red Wings dynasty
1956–1960	Montreal Canadiens first dynasty
1962–1967	Toronto Maple Leafs second dynasty
1965–1969	Montreal Canadiens second dynasty
1972	Fred Shero hires Mike Nykoluk as the first NHL assistant coach.
1976–1979	Montreal Canadiens third dynasty
1980	Herb Brooks coaches Team USA to a 1980 Olympic Gold Medal.
1980–1983	New York Islanders dynasty
1984–1990	Edmonton Oilers dynasty
2001	University of Minnesota–Duluth wins the first NCAA women's hockey championship.
2016	Arizona Coyotes hire Dawn Braid as a skating coach.

GLOSSARY

DYNASTY (DYE-nuh-stee)—a team that wins multiple championships over a period of several years

EVOLVE (i-VAHLV)—when something develops over a long time with gradual changes

FINESSE (fih-NESS)—in hockey, a special skill, such as skating and passing, that doesn't involve hard hitting or rugged play

FRANCHISE (FRAN-chize)—a team that is a member of a sports league or association

HALL OF FAME (HALL UV FAME)—a place where the best and most important people in a certain activity are honored

INSPIRATIONAL (in-spihr-AY-shun-uhl)—causing people to want to do something special or important

SOVIET UNION (SOH-vee-et YOON-yuhn)—a former federation of 15 republics that included Russia, Ukraine, and other nations of eastern Europe and northern Asia; also called the Union of Soviet Socialist Republics (USSR)

STANLEY CUP (STAN-lee CUP)—the trophy that goes to the champions of the National Hockey League every year; the trophy has been around since 1893

READ MORE

Berglund, Bruce. *Big-Time Hockey Records.* North Mankato, MN: Capstone Press, 2022.

Doeden, Matt. *Hockey's Wickedest Goals!* North Mankato, MN: Capstone Press, 2021.

Duling, Kaitlyn. *Women in Hockey.* Lake Elmo, MN: Focus Readers, 2020.

INTERNET SITES

Hockey Hall of Fame
hhof.com

NHL
nhl.com

The Greatest Coaches in Hockey History
ahockeyworld.net/greatest-coaches-hockey-history/

INDEX

ABOUT THE AUTHOR

Shane Frederick has been writing about sports ever since he worked for his high school newspaper in Chippewa Falls, Wisconsin, in the 1980s. For more than 25 years, he has covered college hockey and other sports in Minnesota for multiple publications, winning several awards for his stories. He is the author of more than 40 sports books for kids, including *The Ultimate Collection of Pro Hockey Records, Hockey Stats and the Stories Behind Them*, and *Hilary Knight: Hockey Hero*. A graduate of the University of St. Thomas in St. Paul, Minnesota, Shane and his wife, Sara, have three children.